Christmas in America

David Cohen, Editor & Project Director
Rick Smolan, Associate Director
Mark Rykoff, Managing Editor
Jennifer Erwitt, Associate Editor
Thomas K. Walker, Art Director
J. Curtis Sanburn, Writer

*This book was made possible with
the generous assistance of:*

 Eastman Kodak Co.

The Christmas Eve service at Home Moravian Church in Winston-Salem, North Carolina.

First published 1988 by Collins Publishers, Inc.,
San Francisco.

Copyright © 1988 by Collins Publishers, Inc.

ISBN 0-00-217968-7

Library of Congress Cataloging-in-Publication Data.
Main entry under title: Christmas in America.

Cohen, David, 1955-
Christmas in America.

   1. Christmas—United States—Pictorial works.
I. Smolan, Rick.
II. Title.

GT4986.A1C63 1988
394.2' 68282' 0973   88-9583

Printed in Japan   First printing August 1988

10   9   8   7   6   5   4   3   2   1

Christmas in America

Images of the holiday season by 100 of America's leading photographers

Collins Publishers

James Magdanz

Just when the air turns frosty and the days shrink into darkness, the Christmas season arrives in America. It begins at Thanksgiving—with families, feasts and football. Then, during the next six weeks we shop and decorate, worship and make merry. Our hearts warm in the winter cold. We find compassion for strangers, and we remember there are miracles. Pious or festive or both, we join together in an extraordinary national festival.

Christmas in America is a family album of this festival photographed by one hundred of America's foremost photojournalists. These talented men and women, many veterans of the *Day in the Life of America* project, represent America's leading newspapers and magazines. From Thanksgiving to Epiphany, they scattered across the nation to document how we prepare for, celebrate, survive and clean up after Christmas. Some of them stayed close to home, focusing on their own families and towns. Others went far afield to discover new places and unaccustomed rituals. All together, the photographers took over 150,000 pictures, 150,000 different moments.

The results are as diverse as the American people, as joyous as the season, and as warm and intimate as a family album should be. We hope that you will find some pictures here that capture your holiday memories and feelings, some others that surprise and delight you, and still others that make you pause. Most of all, we hope that you and your family will have a picture perfect Christmas.

B etty Boop tips her hat to Central Park and the start of the Christmas season in the Macy's Thanksgiving Day Parade. Ms. Boop joined the New York parade in 1985.
Photographer:
Kenneth Jarecke
Contact Press Images

Remember me to Herald Square! Snoopy and the Macy's Parade at 34th Street and Broadway, New York City.
Photographer:
Jean-Pierre Laffont, *Sygma*

New Jersey turkey farmer Herbert Ashley introduces grandson Scott to the Christmas crop of birds.
Photographer:
Paul Solomon, *Wheeler Pictures*

Five-pound fruitcakes-to-be ride a conveyor belt past the cherry and almond stations on the assembly line at Grandma's Fruitcake Bakery in Beatrice, Nebraska. The cakes' fragrant essences (bourbon, brandy and rum) have already been stirred into the dough.
Photographer:
Dan White

"His eyes: how they twinkled! his dimples: how merry!
His cheeks were like roses, his nose like a cherry;
His droll little mouth was drawn up like a bow,
And the beard on his chin was as white as the snow."

—*from "A Visit from St. Nicholas" by Clement Clarke Moore, 1823.*

Santas from the Dixie Doodle talent agency in Orange, California, strive for just the right look before heading out to the malls. Santas with genuine beards command three times more pay than those who must don fake whiskers.
Photographer:
Elaine Isaacson, *Orange County Register*

This gathering of Santas marks the kick-off of the Sidewalk Santa Campaign in New York City, sponsored by the Volunteers of America.

New York, like most American cities, hosts dozens of Santas during the holiday season. But in 1948, the Boston city council introduced a resolution asking the mayor to designate an official Saint Nick for the entire city. As one councilman said, "there is a Santa on every corner and the children are beginning to wonder." The request was denied, and the problem of multiple Santas lingers.

These Santas are recruited from the VOA's Men's Rehabilitation Center, which offers job training and alcohol rehabilitation to New York's homeless men. During the Christmas season, they blanket the city, ringing their bells and coaxing quarters and dollar bills from passers by to help feed, clothe and shelter the homeless.
Photographer:
Jeff Jacobson, *Archive*

At the Hutterite community in Norfolk, Connecticut, Susan Barth braves the slush and cold to get some fresh-baked cookies from the communal kitchen.
Photographer:
Brad Clift, *Hartford Courant*

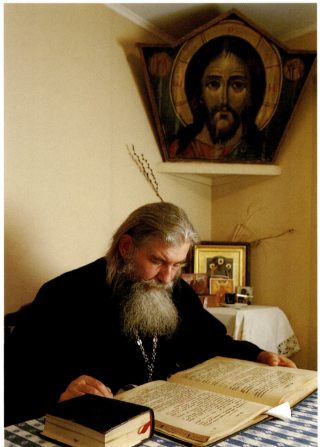

Father Boris Kizenko reads from the Book of Psalms in the rectory of St. Vladimir's Memorial Church in Cassville, New Jersey. According to the Julian calendar used by all Eastern Orthodox churches, Christmas is observed on January 6. *Photographer:* **Nina Barnett**

It's Saturday, December 12 and time for the annual office Christmas party at John Brady Design Consultants, Pittsburgh, Pennsylvania.
Photographer:
Randy Olson, *Pittsburgh Press*

When the posh Topanga Plaza shopping mall in Canoga Park, California, barred the Salvation Army from soliciting donations on its property, the Army's stubborn corps simply moved out to the parking lot entrance.

Cadet Leslye Hall says she got her idea for the pole net from Matthew 4:19: "And He said to them, 'Follow me and I will make you fishers of men.'"

Photographer:
Olga Shalygin, *Los Angeles Daily News*

Volunteers from the Robert H. Schuller Ministries in Garden Grove, California, stuff 15,000 "Merry Christmas" boxes for inmates at the state prison facilities in Chino. Each carton includes a dozen home-baked cookies, a Christmas card, a poem and a prayer.

Photographer:
Rick Rickman, *Orange County Register*

In 1985, a young social worker, Shoshana Arden (behind the table in a red dress), began distributing Christmas presents to needy Philadelphians. By 1987, her gift for gift-giving had become a full-scale community tradition, involving hundreds of donors and volunteers.

Here, Brian J. Woznicki, a 34-year-old computer programmer with cerebral palsy, joins the wrapping party.

"I was with a friend when Shoshana told us about the project," Brian says. "It seemed like a good thing to do, so I came over and offered to do what I could to help. My job is putting the right presents into the right boxes."

Photographer:
Nick Kelsh

Workers prep poinsettia plants for shipment in a football-field-sized greenhouse at Color Spot Nursery in Richmond, California. The midwinter bloomer is a native of central Mexico, where the Aztecs used its red leaves for dye and its sap as a treatment for fever. Seventeenth-century Franciscan friars from Spain began the Mexican tradition of adorning Nativity pageants with banks of poinsettias, which became known as *flores de noche buena*, or flowers of the holy night.

During the 1820s, the United States ambassador to Mexico was an amateur botanist named Joel Poinsett. Fascinated by the red-leafed shrub and its associations with the Nativity, Poinsett sent a few of the plants back to friends in South Carolina, who named the curiosity in his honor.
Photographer:
Kim Komenich, *San Francisco Examiner*

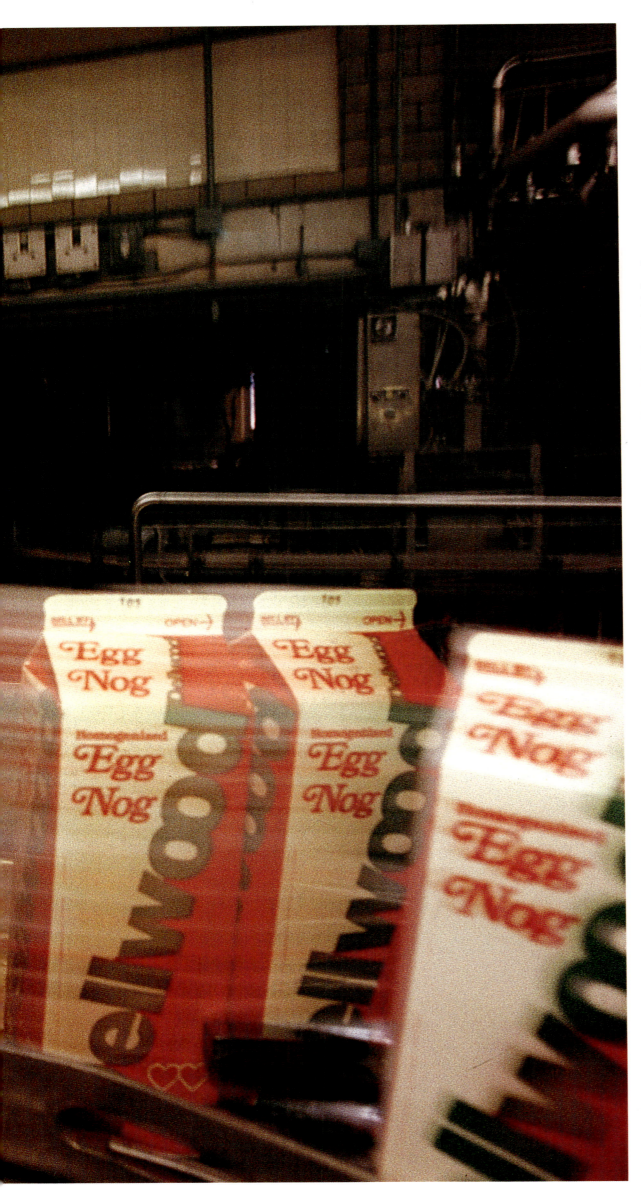

Dellwood Foods of Yonkers, New York, produces over 3,000 gallons of egg nog a day from early November to late December for sale in the New York metropolitan area. Jerry Grosso checks a conveyor belt as cartons speed their way to market.
Photographer:
Christopher Morris
Black Star

White Christmas: At the height of the season, Ervey Morales flocks about 25 trees a day at the Wolfe Nursery in Dallas, Texas.
Photographer:
David Leeson, *Dallas Morning News*

Window dressing: Young Philadelphian Michael Trice peers through his grandmother's holiday decorations.
Photographer:
Sarah Leen, *Philadelphia Inquirer*

Hamlin Farm, near Colebrook, New Hampshire.

Palm Springs, California.

Geoff Manasse, *Aperture*

December in Texas: Ice skaters enjoy the indoor rink at the Galleria shopping mall in suburban Dallas.
Photographer:
Skeeter Hagler, *Dallas Times Herald*

O n a typical December day, over 300,000 parcel-post packages move through the Washington Bulk Mail Center outside Washington, D.C.

Here, Delbert Tullius, a processing equipment technician, unclogs parcels jamming the slide ramp that leads into the high-speed induction sorting system. Parcel volume at the center increases 50 percent during the holiday season, but Tullius says it seems like a lot more.

Photographer:
Bill Ballenberg

I didn't have the Christmas spirit," says mail-man Steve Hudson of Lincoln, Nebraska. "With all the heavy mail and the long hours, you really get tired. So I dressed up as Santa Claus. It gets me through the Christmas season. Everybody loves it. One of my customers started laughing so hard she almost drove into a ditch. Macho guys start acting like little kids.

"Our postmaster doesn't mind; in fact, he enjoys it, mostly because of the public relations. A news-paper reporter asked me if I was having fun. I told him, 'Yeah, but wait until Easter!'"
Photographer:
Kenneth Jarecke
Contact Press Images

I nside every bag is a piece of new clothing, a new toy or game, knitted mittens and candy; all of it gathered, Christmas-wrapped and packed by the Santa Claus Girls of Grand Rapids, Michigan. Phyllis Scanlon, president of the volunteer group, oversees the project, which puts presents under the tree for 11,500 poor children in Kent County.

Three hundred volunteer drivers deliver the gift bags on the Saturday before Christmas.
Photographer:
Lance E. Wynn, *Grand Rapids Press*

E sprit de Christmas: Soldiers from Fort Detrick unload a truckful of gifts in Emmitsburg, Maryland. The packages will be distributed to needy families.
Photographer:
Bill Wood

C apt. Bob Martin of the New Albany, Indiana,
Fire Department restores an old tricycle. The
trike will eventually find its way to a needy child
on Christmas morning.

The fire department's toy restoration and distri-
bution program began 70 years ago; Capt. Martin
has been fixing toys for 28 years.
Photographer:
Gary S. Chapman, *Louisville Courier-Journal*

By his own estimation, Bertil E. Valley is one of the busiest Santas in Seattle. The 74-year-old native of Sweden began his 12 years of ho-ho-hoing after a long vacation in England where he didn't feel like shaving. When Valley returned, a neighbor asked him to impersonate St. Nick for his grandchildren, and the rest is history.

Why does he do it? "The love of children. The smiles, the happiness I see in people. Often, even when I'm in my civilian clothes, children look at me and wonder if I'm Santa Claus. Once my wife and I were in Sweden, shopping in a store, and a little girl looked at me funny and asked her mother if I wasn't *Jultomten*.

"Practice? I didn't have to practice, because I love children, I get a big kick out of them. It's just a matter of listening to what they want Santa Claus to bring them, and then being very careful not to promise anything."

Photographer:
Peter Haley, *Tacoma Morning News Tribune*

Los Angeles, Ca.   Peter Essick

Orange, Ca.   Elaine Isaacson

Wheaton, Md.   Michael S. Wilson

San Francisco, Ca.   Steve Ringman

Richmond, Va.   P. Kevin Morley

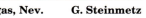

Las Vegas, Nev.   G. Steinmetz

Cypress Gardens, Fla.   George Skene

Since their marriage in 1920, John and Gladys Plemmons of Wichita Falls, Texas, have collected over 1,800 Santas of every description including statues, candleholders, mugs, glasses, dolls, ornaments and bookends.

"My aunt gave me my first Santa, way back before I got married," Gladys says. "Since then, I just always loved Santa, that's all I know. I have every Santa you can think of."
Photographer:
Larry C. Price
Philadelphia Inquirer

A few days before Christmas in Pitkin County, Colorado.
The tepee is home to a mountain couple and their children.

The Merced River in Yosemite National Park on the

Richard Monta, 48, has shuffled in and out of prison most of his life. On Christmas Eve, he was freed from McNeil Island Correctional Center in Washington state, having served 10 years for possession of stolen property as a habitual offender. Released on parole, Monta says he plans to walk the straight and narrow. "I'm not doing life on the installment plan," he says.

Monta (*above*) returns his prison-issued clothing and bedding to a guard station at the prison.

Champagne, tinsel and lots of relatives greet Monta back at his sister's house near Tacoma (*right*). Here, he hugs his nephew, Michael Bolieu and Michael's wife, Ramona, while sister Faye looks on.
Photographer:
Peter Haley, *Tacoma Morning News Tribune*

The Christmas homecoming of the U.S.S. Guadalcanal at Norfolk, Virginia, one week before Christmas. The helicopter assault ship and crew of 800 were returning from a six-month deployment with the Sixth Fleet in the Mediterranean Sea and Persian Gulf.
Photographer:
Karen Kasmauski, *Wheeler Pictures*

Andrew Fiederlein, 9, is the youngest of 400 tuba-tooters at the annual Tuba Christmas concert at Rockefeller Center in New York City.

One hundred cities in the United States and Canada now host tuba choirs at Christmastime, all of them organized by Harvey Phillips, Distinguished Professor of Music at Indiana University. Phillips started the concerts as a tribute to the world's greatest tubaist, William Bell, who was born on Christmas Day, 1902.
Photographer:
Misha Erwitt, *New York Daily News*

A board the Veterans of Foreign Wars float in Fulton, Missouri's annual Christmas parade.
Photographer:
Peter Essick
University of Missouri

I wanted to be with my daughter, Victoria, in the parade. That's important, to do things with your children. And I was a majorette in high school myself," says Jackie Billingslea, 27, dressed as a baton-twirling clown for the Aliquippa, Pennsylvania, Christmas parade. Behind her, Victoria and the rest of the Tylerette Pom-Pom girls march up Franklin Avenue.

Photographer:
Melissa Farlow, *Pittsburgh Press*

While the Snowflake Chorus waits attentively, seven-year-old Kyle Anders delivers his lines as the town crier in the Christmas play at St. Mary's school, New Albany, Indiana.
Photographer:
Pamela K. Spaulding
Louisville Courier-Journal

adison, Wisconsin, had just had its worst snowstorm (14 inches) in years, so they had to close most schools and businesses . . . gee, what a shame!
Photographer:
Zane B. Williams

C hoir kids chatter in Fellowship Hall during
warm-up for the Christmas candlelight service
at the First Presbyterian Church, Haddonfield,
New Jersey.

The baritone on the right, Jamie Barker, 16, has
spina bifida, a paralytic condition that is the most
common birth defect in the United States. After
school, Jamie works as a volunteer at the Bancroft
School for children with special needs.
Photographer:
April Saul, *Philadelphia Inquirer*

The Christmas program, "Mr. Grumpy's Toy Shop," underway at Fairmont Elementary School in New Albany, Indiana.
Photographer:
Pamela K. Spaulding
Louisville Courier-Journal

The stable scene from the children's Christmas program at the United Methodist Church, Spragueville, New York.

The farm animals, shepherds and angels had gathered 'round, and the three wise men had just presented the gold, frankincense and myrrh to the Holy Child, when baby Jesus (played by five-year-old Michael Hartle) decided to wave to his real mother in the audience.

Photographer:
Norm Kerr, *Eastman Kodak*

It's beginning to look a lot like Christmas: The first snowfall of the season delights schoolchildren in Syracuse, New York.
Photographer:
Michael Greenlar, *Picture Group*

"What means that star," the Shepherds said,
"That brightens through the rocky glen?"
And angels, answering overhead,
Sang, "Peace on earth, good-will to men!"
          — from "A Christmas Carol"
            by James Russell Lowell, 1888.

Vincent Fisher, 5, and his sister Toni, 7, share
the stage at the Father Benedict Justice
School in Kansas City, Missouri.
Photographer:
Dan White

Jenny Johnson, 12, is dressed as St. Lucia. According to Swedish custom, she prepares coffee and sweet rolls and, gaily singing the Lucia song, serves breakfast in bed to the rest of the Johnson family in Madison, Wisconsin.

December 13 is known among Swedes as Santa Lucia Day and marks the start of the Swedish Christmas celebration. St. Lucia was a fourth-century Roman beauty martyred when she gave away her considerable dowry to the outlawed Christians. Her unhappy fiancé informed against her, and she was condemned to burn at the stake.
Photographer:
Zane B. Williams

The Christmas Spectacular at New York City's Radio City Music Hall bills itself as "the year's biggest show" casting "the season's warmest glow." As always, the stars of the great stage are the legendary Rockettes, all spit-and-polish precision in the Parade of the Wooden Soldiers.
Photographer:
Dana Fineman, *Sygma*

Young dancers paint themselves into toy soldiers for Act I of the Richmond Ballet's production of *The Nutcracker*.
Photographer:
Joanna B. Pinneo, *Foreign Mission Board*

On Silver Lake near Rochester, Minnesota. Just upstream from the lake, a municipal power plant uses river water to cool its steam turbines. The heated water returns to the river and warms the lake, keeping it free of ice all through Minnesota's deep-freeze winter. As a result, more than 10,000 Canada geese and a troop of ducks shorten their southward migration and spend the winter on Silver Lake's steaming waters.
Photographer:
Joe Rossi
St. Paul Pioneer Press and Dispatch

Dancers wait in the wings for the "Waltz of the Flowers" during the second act of the Richmond Ballet's production of *The Nutcracker*.

Virtually unknown in America until 1954 (when the New York City Ballet introduced a production choreographed by George Balanchine), *The Nutcracker* is now a Christmastime standard for nearly every American ballet company. It is one of the few sure-fire, crowd-pleasing ballets in the dance repertoire, and without it few ballet companies could survive.

Children delight in *The Nutcracker*'s fairy-tale transformations. The ballet is often a child's first serious theater experience, and it has inspired countless youngsters to take ballet lessons with the hope of someday playing a toy soldier, a mouse or even the heroine Clara.

Photographer:
Joanna B. Pinneo
Foreign Mission Board

Costumed members of the Northwest Jet-Skiers Association disrupt the quiet of Puget Sound near Tacoma, Washington, with a strange update on the Santa-and-his-reindeer theme.
Photographer:
Peter Haley, *Tacoma Morning News Tribune*

At age 10, Jerry Falwell wanted a Cushman motor scooter for Christmas, but his parents "thought it was the last thing I needed, reckless as I was."

The energetic preacher who once led the right-wing Moral Majority now spends much of his time at home in Lynchburg, Virginia, where he is pastor of Thomas Road Baptist Church and chancellor of Liberty University. His wife, Macel, decorates their antebellum plantation house every season, including the tree, which comes down promptly on New Year's Day.
Photographer:
Bill Ballenberg

Taking a bough: The Twin Singing Christmas Trees at the First Baptist Church in Orlando, Florida. A tradition since 1980, the trees each hold 210 live ornaments.
Photographer:
George Skene, *Orlando Sentinel*

Alex Joanow, 18, raises the cross skyward after retrieving it from a bayou in Tarpon Springs, Florida.

After reading from the Gospel and sprinkling holy water on the bayou, a bishop of the church hurls the cross into the water. Young men must wait until the cross is in the air before diving after it. According to Greek Orthodox lore, Joanow will be a lucky man for the rest of the year.

The ritual was brought to the United States by Greek immigrants as part of Epiphany Day celebrations held January 6 to commemorate the baptism of Christ.

Photographer:
Seny Norasingh

Small votive candles, or *farolitos*, outline the Inn at Loretto

Sunset lights a Russian olive windrow on the Benson farm in Bigelow, southwestern Minnesota.

"On the night of the 23rd," says photographer Joe Rossi, a native Minnesotan, "it started to rain—freezing rain—through Christmas Eve morning. I took a walk through the pastures that night with the Bensons. I was shooting at a slow shutter speed, 1/15th of a second, hand-held. Everything was becoming so dark, but the ice was catching the remaining sunlight as if it was illuminated from within.

"The other reason I shot the picture was that I was at the end of the roll and I wanted to finish it off before I went in. Even if the shot wasn't good enough to be published, I wanted it for myself."
Photographer:
Joe Rossi, *St. Paul Pioneer Press and Dispatch*

Small votive candles, or *farolitos*, outline the Inn at Loretto
in Santa Fe, New Mexico.

Eduardo Fuss

In the course of the *Christmas in America* project, Kodak, Collins Publishers, WNYC's *Kids America* and the National 4-H Council organized a photo contest for some of America's best young photographers.

When a rare Christmastime snowfall dusted Saguro National Monument near Tuscon, Arizona, sixteen-year-old Alethea Fadala recognized a photo opportunity and snapped this prize-winning shot. For more prizewinners by America's young people, see pages 172, 173.

Photographer:
Alethea Fadala, *National 4-H Council*

As Joseph and Mary, Leroy Martinez and Valerie Medina solemnly accept sanctuary from Sante Fe's Chimayo Mission. For nine nights in December, the Mexican communities of New Mexico stage *Las Posadas*, the traditional reenactment of the journey of Joseph and Mary and their search for a room. The processions unite entire communities for hymns, prayers and feasting.

Photographer:
Tony O'Brien, *Picture Group*

A December evening in Aspen, Colorado. Once a mining town, Aspen struck gold again in the late 1950s as a destination for America's most fashionable skiers.
Photographer:
Paul Chesley, *Photographers/Aspen*

One of the busiest corners in New York overloads two nights before Christmas as shoppers flood the Broadway entrance to Macy's, "The World's Largest Store." The great emporium starred in the 1947 classic, *Miracle on 34th Street*, the Hollywood confection that proved once and for all the existence of Santa Claus.
Photographer:
Jerry Valente

Two sidewalk Santas arrive at the 50th Street subway station en route to their posts on Manhattan's Fifth Avenue.
Photographer:
Misha Erwitt
New York Daily News

Newtok, Alaska

Wailea, Hawaii

Rick Peterson

Loyce and William Willis of Garden Grove, California, spent two days decorating this Honda 1200 Gold Wing motorcycle. Overhead, there's a motorized Santa and sleigh that plays Christmas carols. On the back of the bike is a little Christmas cabin tableau. Willis says he does it for the wide-eyed looks kids give him.
Photographer:
Patrick Tehan, *Orange County Register*

Christmas Day above Mount Daly near Snowmass, Colorado: Winds, light and variable; skies clear; temperature, 20°. "It's like a Christmas present to myself," says commercial balloonist Jake Reyna. "Very steerable, the best possible day we could have up here."
Photographer:
Paul Chesley, *Photographers/Aspen*

The *Mr. Bobb* motors away from the Miami Christmas boat parade with all the top honors. The boat shines with over 14,000 lights ("We lost count," says Mrs. Bobb Messingschlager, the owner's wife). Once, comedian Bob Hope asked if he and his wife, Dolores, could come aboard. A snapshot from their visit to the flashy yacht was reprinted on the Hopes' Christmas card, which was sent out to 6,000 of their friends. *Photographer:*
J. B. Diederich, *Contact Press Images*

Christmas classic: A '57 Chevrolet Bel-Air struts its stuff on Peacock Lane in Portland, Oregon.
Photographer:
Jeffrey Myers, *FPG International*

D orothy and Charles Stitham of Marinwood, California, started tinkering with Christmas decorations in 1959. "Each year we try to add something new," says Dorothy, "but space is becoming a problem.

"In 30 years we've created a lasting holiday tradition. The wide-eyed two year olds of the 1960s have returned with their own kids in the 1980s. For us, this seems to be the way Christmas always was and always will be."
Photographer:
Doug Menuez, *Picture Group*

A drizzly Christmas night in New Castle, Delaware, makes the 240,000
lights covering the Faucher property glow a little more luminously.

The National Christmas Tree and the south portico of the White House glitter on a cold Washington evening. A focal point of the nation's Christmas festival, the tree has been lit by the President every year since 1923. The present tree was permanently planted on the Ellipse in 1973.

Christmas trees weren't always in such favor. The 26th president, Theodore Roosevelt, was a serious conservationist who barred the use of cut trees anywhere in the White House. The ban didn't sit well with his sons, Archie and Quentin, who sneaked a tree into their room anyway. Theodore's cousin Franklin, on the other hand, grew Norway spruces for commercial sale at his Hyde Park, New York, estate.

Mamie Eisenhower set a White House record when she filled her home with 26 Christmas trees in 1959.
Photographer:
Kenneth Garrett

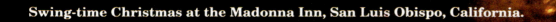
Swing-time Christmas at the Madonna Inn, San Luis Obispo, California.

Mattie McCargo of Detroit hosts a party on the last day of *Kwanza*, the seven-day midwinter celebration of African culture and community in America. *Kwanza* (from the Kiswahili word meaning "first" or "first fruits") was started by a Los Angeles teacher of Swahili, Ron Karenga, in the early 1970s. Derived from African harvest festivals, the modern celebration stresses seven principles to guide African-American families: Unity, self-determination, collective work and responsibility, cooperative economics, purpose, creativity, and faith.

The candleholder (*kinara*) in front of McCargo counts the principles—and the days of the festival—with its red, green and black candles.

Photographer:
William DeKay, *Detroit Free Press*

Veteran photographer Jack Corn returned to the family farm in Sumner County, Tennessee, where he found his grandson Austin fascinated by whirring, tinkling star-chimes. Andrew Corn, Austin's father, shares the candlelight.
Photographer:
Jack Corn, *Chicago Tribune*

Dressed for church on Christmas Eve, the Mortons of Warsaw, Virginia, and their granddaughter Katie first open one present each. They save the rest for Christmas morning.
Photographer:
Kenneth Garrett

Grade-schoolers harmonize at a Christmas concert at the Neil Blaisdell Auditorium in Honolulu.
Photographer:
Rick Smolan
Collins Publishers

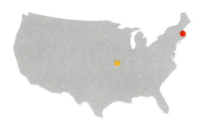

T wo days before Christmas, Shirley Karnovsky tries to console a call-in at the Samaritans suicide prevention office in Boston.

According to Karnovsky, and contrary to popular belief, there are actually fewer suicides during the holidays, but it's the time of year when family and financial problems can cause otherwise stable people to *feel* suicidal. "The calls are more serious during Christmas," she says.

Photographer:
Stan Grossfeld, *Boston Globe*

At the University of Missouri, pianist Michelle Werner leads the caroling at Alpha Gamma Delta during their house decorating party. The idea is to get the girls—and the house itself—in the Christmas spirit before exams start next week. *Photographer:*
Peter Essick, *University of Missouri*

The Rowley family invited photographer Nick Kelsh to spend Christmas Eve and Christmas morning with them at their home in Philadelphia. Their hospitality made possible this chronicle of a family Christmas, spread over the next few pages. Photographer Kelsh took the holiday portrait below in front of the family tree: (*from left to right*) Jim, Karen, Peter, Monica, Rachel, Alice, Karen, Hannah and Abigail.

At 7:00 p.m. on Christmas Eve, Jim and Karen (*right, above*) gathered the children around the dining room table to light the last Advent candle. At midnight, they placed a figure of Jesus in the middle of the candles.

After the kids went to bed, Dad climbed onto the roof and rapped on the shingles with a broom (*right, below*), hoping to convince the youngest kids that reindeer were shuffling about.

Photo essay by Nick Kelsh

The Rowley living room at 6:45 a.m., Christmas morning.

And the Rowley living room at 7:45 a.m., Christmas morning.

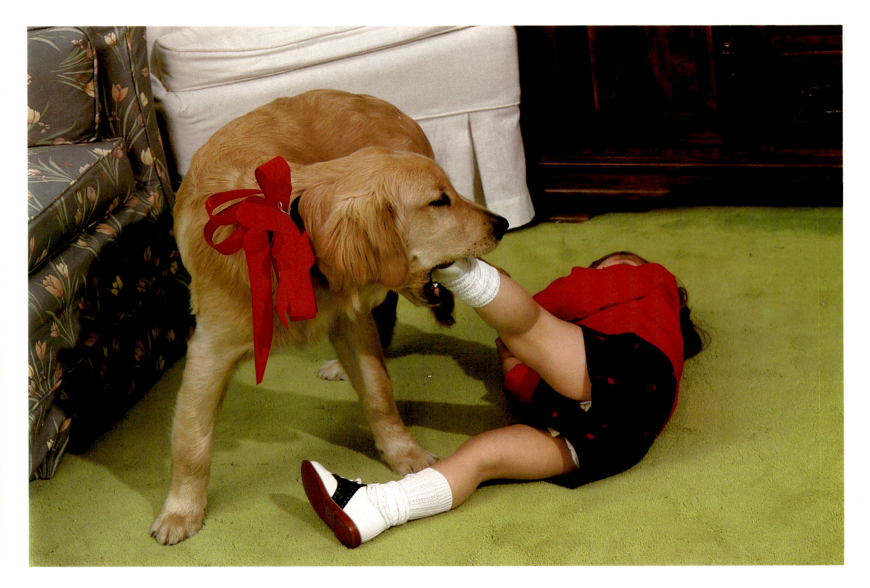

R uff-housing: Golden Retriever Clancy and his playmate Patrick Dymond on Christmas Day in Pennsauken, New Jersey.
Photographer:
Gerald Seone Williams, *Philadelphia Inquirer*

When the children have been good,
That is, be it understood,
Good at meal-times, good at play,
Good all night, and good all day,
They shall have the pretty things
Merry Christmas always brings.
                    —*English proverb, 1850.*

S eth Harvey, 6, of Manchester, Massachusetts, is rewarded with that great old standby, a Lionel train set.
Photographer:
David Alan Harvey, *National Geographic*

Curtis Battle has been taking care of Cynthia Forrest and her one-year-old son Brandon for several months, though it's getting harder and harder. Throughout the month of December, they've been living in his car. Here, they're having Christmas dinner "at home" in a parking lot in Venice Beach, California.

Formerly a fast-food restaurant manager in Washington, D.C., Battle has been looking for work in Los Angeles for four months. Earlier in the day, the family had lunch at the Union Rescue Mission in downtown Los Angeles, where volunteers gave Brandon some candy canes and a doll.
Photographer:
Rick Rickman, *Orange County Register*

Christmas Quartet: Three-month-old David, Kathryn, Benjamin and Gregory Vanderwoude line up on the laps of their parents, Chris and Phil, for this Christmas Day portrait in Grand Rapids, Michigan.

Early morning near Bigelow, Minnesota.

Every year, Russell and Eleanor Wimbish bring a Christmas tree to the Vietnam Veterans Memorial in Washington, D.C. The tree is for Eleanor's son, William Stocks, an Army sergeant who died in a helicopter crash in Vietnam on February 13, 1969.
Photographer:
Sal Lopes

At CNN Center in Atlanta, graphic artist Jim Powell works through Christmas Day preparing the "over-the-shoulder box" visible on the monitors. At broadcast time, the artwork will appear over the shoulder of the anchorperson who, in this case, will be reporting on Christmas festivities aboard U.S. Navy ships patrolling the Persian Gulf.
Photographer:
Scott Robinson
Atlanta Constitution and Journal

In 1776, Christmas feasting and drinking was considered by many colonists to be a decadent European tradition. On the night of December 25, British and Hessian troops stationed in Trenton, New Jersey, were so preoccupied with holiday revels, in fact, that they failed to post the necessary guards. It was an oversight that helped General Washington and his army rout the garrison the following morning after a surreptitious crossing from the Pennsylvania side of the Delaware River.

Washington's daring raid is reenacted every year on Christmas Day by the citizens of Bucks County, Pennsylvania.

Photographer:
Michael Mancuso
The Times (Trenton, N. J.)

A farmhouse along the White River in Meeker, Colorado. With temperatures hovering around -20° F, moisture from the river freezes into a smoky haze of ice particles.
Photographer:
James Balog

At the Skyline Convalescent Hospital in San Jose, California, Corinne Patterson, 85, spends the morning of December 16 filling in a crossword puzzle. Corinne has no immediate family, and her affairs are managed by a social worker.

Corinne looks forward to the decoration contests, the Christmas Eve party and the traditional Christmas dinner that will enliven the quiet hospital in the days ahead.
Photographer:
Judy Griesedieck, *San Jose Mercury News*

The dayes are very short, the year grows old,
Come, make a blazing fire, the weather is cold,
And fill up a full cup of nut brown beere,
Let's thaw our noses and our hearts upcheere,
For mery Christmas comes but once a year.
                        —*English proverb, 1693.*

A one-horse open sleigh glides across a meadow in central Vermont.
Photographer:
Ira Block, *Image Bank*

Dusk in Madison, Wisconsin.

Juan Nardo spends part of Christmas Day sweeping the ballroom at
Miami Beach's famous Fontainebleau Hotel.

New York's Old Westbury Gardens await the arrival of warmer days.
Photographer:
Elizabeth Billhardt

It's 2:30 a.m., December 25, and Old St. Nick is worn out. With good reason. He has to deliver gifts to children all around the world. And, despite the skepticism of a highly skeptical, highly commercial age, he must embody all the goodwill, generosity and optimism of America's Christmas season. It's a tough job, but yes, Virginia, there is a Santa Claus.
Photographer:
P. Kevin Morley
Richmond Times-Dispatch and News Leader

In 1987 when the New York Giants won the Super Bowl, the top tiers of the Empire State Building blushed blue and white from dusk to dawn. Every Easter week, the 102-story skyscraper beams yellow and white. On Columbus Day, it's red, white and green; and from Halloween to Thanksgiving, New York's famous pinnacle glows in autumnal shades of red, orange and yellow. In all, the building heralds 14 regular holidays with its color-coordinated crown of light. After the red and green of Christmas, as seen here from the Pan Am building, a switch to pure white light ushers in the New Year.
Photographer:
Torin Boyd, *Gamma*

Storefront in Hermann, Missouri.

Sponsors and Contributors

Thanks to:

Sponsors
Eastman Kodak Co.
K mart
Pan Am
Federal Express

Contributors
Adobe Systems, Inc.
Aldus Corporation
Apple Computer, Inc.
Barneyscan Corporation
Church of the Nativity
Dr. Robert H. Schuller & the Crystal Cathedral
   Congregation
Electronic Publishing Services
Express Package Systems, Inc.
Greater Houston Convention & Visitors Bureau
Grosvenor House Apartments
Kids America
Lighthouse Church of God & Christ
Lightspeed
L' Image Photo Lab, Inc.
Living Videotext Corporation
Lundeen & Associates
Metropolitan Life Insurance
Microprint
Mission Communities of Holy Family Parish
Moniterm Corporation
National 4-H Council
Our Lady of Guadalupe Church
Pallas Photo Lab, Inc.
Pan Am Building
Spofford Juvenile Center
St. Catherine's Church of Greenwich
SuperMac Technology
The Big Apple Circus
WNYC

Jeff Abbaticcio
Don Abood
Tom Adkinson
Jeff Allen
Bob Ambriano
Walter Anderson
Susan Andrews
Rich Andrews
Joseph Antonini
Al Apodaca
Ofelia Aquino
Ramon Araya
Bonnie Arnold
Allen Bachman
Monica Baltz
Anna Maria Bambara
Martha Bardach
Richard & Diana Barker
   & Family
Jeanne Bayer
Fr. Albert Bauman,
   O.S.B.
Dennis Beal
J. L. & Juanita Beasley
David Beckwith
David Benson Family
Jesse Birnbaum
Fr. Jose Maria Blanc
Britt Blaser
Herb Bleiweiss
Gene Blumberg
Ann Marie Boivie
Rachel Bolton
Liz Bond
Angela Bordon
Erik Boyd
Linda Boyes
Roger Brashears, Jr.
Clinton Breckridge
Kandes Bregman
Bart Brittain
Wallace Bronner
Deacon John Brooks
Thomas Brown
Marisa Bulzone
Diane Burns
Don Cable
Wendy Cacacie
Anthony Calcagno
Robert Cameron
Todd Cameron
Woodfin Camp
David Carriere
John Mack Carter
Mike Cerre
Maya Chernyak
Mary Chesterfield
Judy Ann Christensen
Albert Chu
Rachel Cobb

Gail Cohen
Hannnah & Norman
   Cohen
Christophe Colbert
Frank Collins
Sandy Colton
Debby Comiskey
Vicki Comiskey
Jim Connett
Sue Contois
Jennifer Cook
Ed Cooper
Patrick & Dorothy
   Corbett
Jim Cornacchia
Jennifer Corrigan
Merrill Creekmore
Beth Crowell
Larrie Curry
Steven Curtis
Jim Dau
Alan Davies
Jim Davis
Larry Davis
Bob DeCarlo
Kelly Decker
Mary Anne Decker
Cliff Deeds
Ray DeMoulin
Linda Dennery
Tom & Mary Jane Devine
Betty Dibartolomeo
Alan DiMarco
Chickie Dioguardi
Fred & Tuni Dixon
   & Family
Ron Dogey
Patrick Doherty
Miguel Dominguez, Ph.D.
Leon Donach
Craig Donahue
Debbie Donnelly
John Dougherty
Gene & Gayle Driskell
D.R. Ricky Duling
John Durniak
Van Mol Dye
Oscar Dystel
Mary Dawn Earley
Steve Edelman
Maura Eggan
Lynne Eich
Pat Ellerby
Connie Enzminger
Elliott Erwitt
Barbara Essick
Craig Evans
Bernard Fagan, S.J.
Bill Farley
Craig Farnum

Peter Feild
Vern Feild
Harlan Felt
Lisa Ferdinandsen
Mr. & Mrs. Ivan
   Filiatrault
Louise Finn
Frank Finnegan
Peter Fish
Peter Fishback
George Fisher
Flavio Flaviani
Dick Fleming
Charlotte Folkening
Paulette and Lazlo Fono
Ken Fossan
John Frank
Paulette Galle
Thomas A. Gara
Jesus J. Garcia
Simone Gaudin
Tom Geddie
Kent Gerken
Tara S. Gilani
Emmit Glanz
Louis Glazer
Michael Goldstein
Manuel Gombos
Linda Gomez
Sr. Angelina Gonzales
Emerson Goodwin
Jim Gordon
D. Gorton
George Greenfield
Millie Greig
Elaine Griffin
Tony Grigsbee
Bernard W. Groff
Joan Grossman
Don Guglielmino
Joe Guttierez
Annette Gutzmiedl
Catherine Gysin
Bernard Hagan
Dr. Clara Hale
Maj. C. C. Hall
Gregory Hall
Claus Halle
Cynthia Hallex
Steve Hansen
Sheila Hanson
Dean Hanson
Steve Haslett
Barbara Hawkins
Dina Hazan
Bonnie L. Heintz
Linda Hendrix
Manuel Hernandez
Andy Hertzfeld
John Hetterick

Dixie Hibbard
Preston Hibbard
Todd Hickson
James Higa
Kevin Hildebrand
Mike Holm
Twyla Holt
Ritchie Horowitz
Peter Howe
Cynthia Westbrook Hu
Peggie Ioppini
John Rice Irwin
Vern Iuppa
Charlie Jackson
Janice James
Joanne Jessie
Laura Jobin
Steve Jobs
Valtrey Johnson
Sr. Ramona Johnson
Charles Jones
Bill Joy
Larry Kanter
Jack Kardys
Susan Kare
Sheila Karnovsky
The Kell Family
The Reverends Kathy
  & Colin Kerr-Carpenter
Will Ketterson
Sharon Klaschka
Doreen & Fritz Klatt
Emily Klenk
Steve Knowlton
Jan Knox
Kent Kobersteen
Jeff Kriendler
Andrew Kruger
Bill Kuykendall
Tom Kyle
Mr. & Mrs. Philippe
  Lacoudre
Eliane Laffont
Ray Lake
Linda Lamb
Jerry Lawrence
Shari Lawrence
Mr. & Mrs. David
  Leading
John LeBosquet
John & Pam Leckie
Jim Leonard
Carleen Levasseur
Andy Levine
Chet Lewis
Ted Lewis
Ken Lieberman
Leslie Anne Liedtka
Nancy Littell
Jim Little & Family

Robin Lord
Barbara Loren
Mike Lotif
Patty Lucas
Glendon Lufkin
Tim Lundeen
Carolyn Mack
Judi Magann
Al Mandel
Marcy Mankoff
Joyce Mantyla
Thom Marchionna
Mike Marshall
Horace Marshall Family
Meg Martescello
Linda Mather
Joyce Matsumoto
Jed Mattes
Richard & Lucienne
  Matthews
James & Julie Matthias
Pat McCorkell, S.J.
Fallon McElliot
Carol McElroy
Pat McFerren
John & Judy McGarvey
Dan McGill
Warren McGlade
John McGlade
D. Pat McGuire
Mary McPherson
Naomi Medearis
Edwin Mellett
Lynda Mendez
Stan Menscher
Eric Meskauskis
Maria Miller
Melanie Miller
Richard Miller
Marla Milne
Pam Miracle
Deborah L. Mirams
Nancy Miscia
Ann Marie Molders
Art Mont
Richard Monta
Edmund Morales
Lynn Moratzka
Daize Biscaro Moreira
Stacy Morgan
Denise Morse
Ann Moscicki
Bruce Mowery
Robert Mullen
Deborah Munch
Lon Murphy
Nancy Nabors
Thomas Nigolian
Nick Nishida
Diane Norman

Kathy O'Connell
Dan O'Shea
Masaaki Okada
Clara & Elmer Olanna
Henri & Rita Olanna
Tony Oppenheim
Larry Orfaly
Celia Organista
Ava Osle
Paul Otomo
Paula Padilla
Richard Palazzo
Liz Palladino
Rusty Pallas
Rick Pappas
Seth Parelman
Larry Parkin
Dixie Marshall Parks
Dorraine Pate
Tyler Peppel
Liz Perle
Kenneth "Aku" Perreira
Naiken Perunal
Tatiana Petrovsky
The Reverend Peter
  Phavasiri, O.M.I.
David Pilgrim & Staff
Junette Pinkney
Jeanne & Larry Pinneo
Roger Pisani
Teobaldo H. Pla
Tom Plaskett
Robert Pledge
John Poimiroo
Elizabeth Pope
Carol Poston
Alison Pratt
Dan Procopio
Paul Pruneau
Jeff Pruss
Cherie Quaintance
Liz Quick
Eli Reed
Janet Reed
Alice M. Reid
Myra R. Reid
Dr. Lucy Reifel
Thomas P. Reilly
Ed Reingold
Andrew Rich
Lynda Richardson
Jan Roberts
Norman Roberts
Hugh & Rachel Rodgers
Robyn Roessler
Capt. John Rondon
Michael R. Rondou
Jack Rose
Terry Rosen
Jim Rowley

Lt. Noel Roy
Nancy Ruggeiro
Pat Ryan
Thomas Rykoff
Nola Safro
Sanjay Sakhuja
Janet Sakhuja
Marianne Samenko
Will & Marta Sanburn
Daniel Sare
David Sayre
Al Scamahorne
Tony Scaturro
Steve Scheier
Fred Scherrer
Cliff Schiappa
Bob Schneider
Kai Schuler
Marilyn Scofield
John Scully
Stuart Seaborn
Debbie Nye Sembler
Deborah Semel
Anne Seto
Kay Sexton
Neil & Karen Shakery
Laura Shultz
Mitch Silverberg
Joanne Sinnot
Doug Sleeter
Dorothea Smith
Peter Smith
Burrell Smith
Temple Smith
Tim Smith
Suzanne Soulié
Joe Spada
Mary Ellen Spanakos
Phil Sperr
David Spindler
Lynn Spivak
Jean Spivey
Lee Stalker
Dawn Stefan
Michelle Stephenson
Robert Stevens
Andy Stewart
Jim Stockton
Carlock Stooksbury
Blanche Streeter
Mary Strutz
Dick Stum
Danny Stupka
Ralph Subbiando
Peter Sutch
Rick Swig
Meg Switzgable
Jon Tandler
Christina A. Tasley
Michael Tchao

Mark Terry
Charles Thomas
Robert Tillman, S.J.
Jan Tipton
Diane Todd
Lynne & Margaret Tolley
Craig Tolman
Hipolito Torres
Anthony Totorici
Bill Tracy
Jean Tracy
The Troupers
Kim Tucker
Karen Tucker
Ruth Velozo
Liza Vicini
John Wade
Mr. & Mrs. James
  Waldron
Ruth Walsh
John Warnock
Greg Watkins
Dr. Jan Welle
Michael Wellman
Eric Weyenberg
Paul E. Wheeler
Ann White
Mr. & Mrs. Albert
  Whitehat
Diane Whitehurst
James Joseph Whiteley
Betty H. Willett
Michael Williams
  & Family
Ruth Williams Bennett
Joseph Wilson
Dave Winer
Philip Wong
Cathy Workman
Peter & Carolan
  Workman
Tom Wrubel
Chris Wurst
Amy Yamasaki
Mary Elizabeth Yost
Lisa Young
Bruce Young
Heidi Zimmerman

Staff

**Editor &
   Project Director**
David Cohen

Associate Director
Rick Smolan

Managing Editor
Mark Rykoff

Associate Editor
Jennifer Erwitt

Art Director
Thomas K. Walker
GRAF/x

Writer
J. Curtis Sanburn

Assignment Editors
Torin Boyd
Devyani Kamdar
Ronald Pledge

Picture Editors
Bernard Boutrit
Woodfin Camp & Assoc.
Sandra Eisert
San Jose Mercury News
Frank Fournier
Contact Press Images
George Olson
Tom Porter
Orange County Register
George Wedding
Sacramento Bee

Production Director
Stephanie Sherman

Design Assistant
Dale Horstman

Copy Editors
Dorian Gossy
Amy Wheeler

Publicity Director
Patti Richards

Sponsorship Director
Cathy Quealy

Sales Director
Carole Bidnick

Finance Director
Stanford Hays

Sales Assistant
Kate Kelly

Office Manager
Lew Stowbunenko

Researchers
Laura Bleiberg
Clio McNicholl
Gloria Smolan

Lawyers
E. Gabriel Perle
New York
William Coblentz
San Francisco

**William Collins Sons &
Co., Ltd**.
F. Ian Chapman
Chairman
George Craig
Vice Chairman
Sonia Land
Group Finance Director

**Dai Nippon Printing
Co., Ltd.**
Ryo Chigira
Toshihiko Miyazaki
Yukio Yoshida
Takashi Ishikawa
Kosuke Tago
Kikuo Mori
Yuichiro Sato
Yoshiyasu Kosugi
Kimio Honda

Christmas in America was entirely designed and produced on an Apple Macintosh II computer equipped with a Supermac Trinitron Monitor and Dataframe XP-60 hard disks. The images were input with a Barneyscan and output on a Linotronic 300 printer. Project software included Aldus Pagemaker, Living Videotext MORE, and Microsoft Works. We gratefully acknowledge the assistance of Microprint and the companies listed on the previous pages for their generous contribution to this book.